Leading
Common Worship
Intercessions

Leading *Common Worship* Intercessions

A Simple Guide

Doug Chaplin

CHURCH HOUSE
PUBLISHING

Church House Publishing
Church House
Great Smith Street
London SW1P 3AZ

ISBN 978–0–7151–4200–4

Published 2009 by Church House Publishing

The opinions expressed in this book are those of the author and do not
necessarily reflect the official policy of the General Synod or The
Archbishops' Council of the Church of England.

Printed in England by CPI Bookmarque, Croydon CR0 4TD

Contents

Contents

Foreword

Leading worshippers in corporate public prayer is a vital ministry within the Christian Church. During the past generation, the nature of intercessory prayer in worship has changed. We have seen a welcome move away from exclusively clergy-led prayer to intercessions prepared and led by representatives of the whole people of God, and we have begun to explore more fully the place of silence, music and multi-sensory elements in prayer.

Those who lead intercessions almost always refer to the enormous privilege of leading others in prayer. But privileges carry responsibilities – in preparation and in delivery. And for each intercessor, however experienced, there is always the question 'how might I do this as well as possible?'

Doug Chaplin is well qualified to tackle this question. In this 'how to' guide, he draws on his extensive experience as a parish priest and trainer, both within his diocese and for *Praxis*. Offering clear, sensible, down-to-earth, yet creative advice, Doug unpacks the principles behind corporate intercession (not least that an intercessor is one who leads others in prayer, rather than praying in front of other people!) and provides helpful routes through the maze. He addresses the important issues of content, style and grammar and shows through a raft of well-chosen 'worked examples' how variety can be achieved within the patterns of prayer found in *Common Worship*.

This is a book containing wisdom both for those who come to lead intercessions for the first time, and for those who are seasoned campaigners.

I am delighted to be able to commend this timely guide as one of a number of resources supporting the Liturgical Commission's *Transforming Worship* initiative. My hope and prayer is that it will be well used as we continue to make 'supplications, prayers, intercessions and thanksgivings for everyone' (1 Timothy 2.1).

Peter Moger
Secretary to the Liturgical Commission and
Worship Development Officer

1

Introduction

This short guide is intended to help you lead other people in prayer. I hope it will be useful to all those who lead prayer in their churches and gatherings, however long you have been doing it. However, I have tried to start from the very beginning for those who have no experience and build up to more creative material for those who have begun to stretch their wings. If you have been asked to lead prayers in your church for the first time and have no idea where or how to start, then this book is for you – particularly its opening chapters – before you progress to more adventurous ways of doing things later in the book. If you have been leading intercessions for some time and want to explore how to develop them further, in different ways, and in various contexts, then this book is also for you – particularly its later chapters – although you might well find it helpful to rehearse the basic underlying principles in its early sections.

Nearly every time I have presided at an act of worship in another church (often one in a vacancy), I have asked a churchwarden what that congregation does at various points in the service, including the prayers of intercession. I have nearly always been given the same answer: 'Oh, we just do it the normal way.' It is astonishing just how many and varied the 'normal' ways of the Church of England are! What is normal in one place is quite new or strange in another. I hope this guide will be of use across many congregations, and not only within the Church of England, but it is impossible to cater for every local variation. I hope, however, that most churches, and especially those joining in *Common Worship*, will be able easily to recognize their own practice.

I have written this guide as a 'how to' manual. It contains some sample forms of the intercessions, practical guidance for carrying out this ministry, and some further ideas for you to explore. It may, therefore, like many 'how to' guides, seem more prescriptive than it is intended to be. What is offered here are guidelines for good practice, and the starting point from which to develop your own good practice. Among all the detailed suggestions, however, there is one piece of advice that needs to come first, head and shoulders above everything else, and is essentially the only 'rule' in this book. **You are leading people in prayer, not praying in front of other people**. The congregation don't need to enjoy your eloquence, admire your deep and orthodox theology, or take pleasure in the fine sound of your wonderfully clear voice. They need to be engaged in prayer.

Anything else that is said in the booklet seeks to support that fundamental point. It is about helping you, as a leader of people's prayers, actually to lead them in their own praying.

2

A word about prayer

Nearly everything in this book is practical, and there are many other guides around to explain the theology and theory. However, it seems important to include a short word about the Church's understanding of prayer. There is a large range of activities that can come under that heading, but there is something characteristically Christian about corporate intercession. According to St Matthew's Gospel, Jesus said: 'If two of you agree on earth about anything you ask, it will be done for you by my Father in heaven. For where two or three are gathered in my name, I am there among them' (Matthew 18.19–20). When he taught people to pray, that prayer began 'Our Father in heaven' (Matthew 6.9) and continued with petitions for God's kingdom and human needs. In both cases, prayer is something done together with at least one other person and includes prayers of asking, such as 'Give us today our daily bread'. Jesus wants his followers to live with a deep and radical trust in God, and he wants them to live as a new family. The pattern of prayer he teaches is one that joins both these themes: seeking God's kingdom in prayer and action is something that is done together, because in God's kingdom we will live together.

The significance of prayer is highlighted in the *Common Worship* baptism and confirmation services by the provision of prayers of intercession as the first activity for the newly initiated. The guidance note says that 'Such prayers draw the newly baptized into the praying Church of which they are now a part. It may be appropriate for the newly baptized to introduce sections of these prayers.'[1] First, prayer is a foundational activity of the Church; secondly, it is one of the great privileges of the baptized to be able to pray – to call God 'Father' and to exercise the priestly responsibility of the Church to intercede for all creation. The Spirit, given in baptism and renewed in confirmation, is the one who enables us to call out 'Abba, Father' (Galatians 4.6) and who also 'intercedes for the saints according to the will of God' (Romans 8.27). It is an essential part of the gift of the Spirit that through the Spirit God enables us to pray. One of the very important features of contemporary church life is the recovery of this sense of the calling of all the baptized, not only the ordained, to share in Christ's ministry. Praying, and helping others to pray, is one of the characteristic ways baptism makes a difference to our lives as God calls us to share the priestly ministry of Christ's intercession for all God's creation.

We learn much about prayer simply through praying with one another. That may begin at home, or in school, as well as in church. Leading intercessions is one of the ways we support others, not only by helping them to pray together then and there in church, but also by feeding their life of personal prayer. Traditionally, Anglican prayer has been fed and nurtured by the words and phrases of the Prayer Book and other liturgies. These still provide a significant part of the vocabulary of prayer that we can draw on, but those who lead prayer are continually enlarging, enriching, and updating the repertoire of phrases and themes everyone can draw on in personal prayer.

Preparation is important in all this. There's an apocryphal story of a priest who decided that to make a little bit of free space in a very full and busy week he would use some of his sermon preparation time to relax, and risk extemporizing his Sunday evening sermon. After all, he reasoned, the congregation was quite small. He realized to his horror as he began the service that the bishop had just come in quietly and was sitting at the back of the church. This panicked him, and his sermon was, quite frankly, truly dreadful. At the door afterwards he apologized: 'Bishop, I'm sorry about the sermon. Tonight I was relying on the Holy Spirit, but next week I shall do better.'

People sometimes take the view that the inspiration of the Holy Spirit is synonymous with spontaneity. After all, Jesus says: 'Say whatever is given you at that time, for it is not you who speak, but the Holy Spirit' (Mark 13.11). However, he is very clear in the context that 'at that time' is when the disciples are being put on trial for their faith. I certainly do not want to denigrate spontaneous prayer; it has an important and vital place, particularly in small groups. Nonetheless, past generations were trained in speaking in a way in which our sound-bite culture is not, and most of us will benefit from significant preparation and writing. The Holy Spirit can and does work through careful reflection, alone at a desk, table, or computer, as much as in front of others. Preparation is about putting prayer as well as thought into the prayers. The remainder of this book is intended to guide that practical and prayerful work of preparation.

3

The basic pattern

The most common pattern of intercession is one we have come to
know first from the *Alternative Service Book 1980*, and now from
Common Worship. It has five main sections, together with a separate
beginning and ending.[2] Those sections are:

- ¶ The Church of Christ
- ¶ Creation, human society, the Sovereign and those in authority
- ¶ The local community
- ¶ Those who suffer
- ¶ The communion of saints.

Many people find it helpful to get this basic structure right, and to keep
it fairly consistent, since familiarity will help people join in. Everyone
knows what's coming, and also that the main areas of people's
concerns will be covered. Without a structure like this, someone might
start off praying for the sick, for instance, while a member of the
congregation is wondering whether they'll ever get round to praying for
a country recently affected by an earthquake. A common structure
helps participation, although there may be occasions when it's clearly
right to do something different. A structure also acts as a basic checklist
for you when you are planning the intercessions.

The *Common Worship* sample text

Here is one of the most familiar forms of the prayers from *Common
Worship*.[3] You will see this follows the basic thematic structure
outlined above.

> In the power of the Spirit and in union with Christ,
> let us pray to the Father.
>
> Almighty God, our heavenly Father,
> you promised through your Son Jesus Christ
> to hear us when we pray in faith.

Strengthen *N* our bishop and all your Church in the service of
 Christ,
that those who confess your name may be united in your truth,
live together in your love, and reveal your glory in the world.

Bless and guide *Elizabeth our Queen*;
give wisdom to all in authority;
and direct this and every nation in the ways of justice
and of peace;
that we may honour one another, and seek the common good.

Give grace to us, our families and friends, and to all our neighbours,
that we may serve Christ in one another, and love as he loves us.

Comfort and heal all those who suffer in body, mind, or spirit . . .;
give them courage and hope in their troubles;
and bring them the joy of your salvation.

Hear us as we remember those who have died in the faith
of Christ . . .;
according to your promises,
grant us with them a share in your eternal kingdom.

Rejoicing in the fellowship of [*N and of*] all your saints,
we commend ourselves and the whole creation to your
unfailing love.

Merciful Father
accept these prayers
for the sake of your Son
our Saviour Jesus Christ. Amen.

Used with a response

This set of intercessions is usually used with this familiar response:

Lord, in your mercy
hear our prayer.

Responses help break up the prayers and, by keeping them in shorter
sections, help people to concentrate. They also provide a clear way for
people to join in vocally. There are other familiar responses that can be
used instead of this one. (See page 32.)

Patterns and structures are important throughout *Common Worship.* This pattern of intercession has its own place in the wider structure of the service:

¶   Gathering
¶   Liturgy of the Word
¶   Liturgy of the Sacrament
¶   Dismissal.

It does not, therefore, have to do everything on every occasion. Praise, penitence and thanksgiving, among other things, are well catered for elsewhere. What the rest of this guide does is explore ways of building on this and other patterns, developing them a step at a time.

4

Using the basic pattern (1)

There are two ways in which this basic example can be used in practice. Both versions provide slightly different patterns that can be adapted for other sets of words. The first owes something to what Anglicans have inherited from *The Book of Common Prayer*, in which a range of biddings (invitations to pray) preceded a long and uninterrupted prayer – 'The Prayer for the Church Militant'. This pattern makes use of a set of simple statements, so that each section has the following structure:

¶ Statements of what we are praying for
¶ Silence
¶ Prayer
¶ Response.

This pattern is demonstrated in the following example.

A fully worked out example

In the power of the Spirit and in union with Christ,
let us pray to the Father.

Almighty God, our heavenly Father,
you promised through your Son Jesus Christ
to hear us when we pray in faith.

We pray for Archbishop Rowan's meeting with the Pope. We pray for our partners in Berlin, and their preparations for the *Kirchentag*,[4] and for continuing movement towards unity among Christians.

Short silence

Strengthen *N* our bishop and all your Church in the service of Christ,
that those who confess your name may be united in your truth,
live together in your love, and reveal your glory in the world.

Lord, in your mercy
hear our prayer.

We pray for continuing efforts to bring peace in the Middle East, and for the people of Iraq and the rebuilding of their society in peace. [We pray] for all those whose lives are lived in fear of tyranny and violence.

Short silence

Bless and guide Elizabeth our Queen; give wisdom to all in
    authority;
and direct this and every nation in the ways of justice and of peace;
that we may honour one another, and seek the common good.

Lord, in your mercy
hear our prayer.

We pray for all those returning to education after the summer holidays, especially for the staff of St James's school, and its place in our community.

Short silence

Give grace to us, our families and friends, and to all our neighbours, that we may serve Christ in one another, and love as he loves us.

Lord, in your mercy
hear our prayer.

We pray for all those in the nursing homes of our parish, and for
    all who are sick,
especially . . .

A list of names follows, then a short silence

Comfort and heal all those who suffer in body, mind, or spirit;
give them courage and hope in their troubles;
and bring them the joy of your salvation.

Lord, in your mercy
hear our prayer.

We give thanks for the life of Jane Smith, and all who have recently died. We call to mind those whose anniversaries of death fall at this time, especially John Brown.

Short silence

Hear us as we remember those who have died in the faith of Christ;
according to your promises,
grant us with them a share in your eternal kingdom.

Lord, in your mercy
hear our prayer.

In silence let us offer our own prayers to our heavenly Father.

Short silence

Rejoicing in the fellowship of the Blessed Virgin Mary and
   all your saints,
we commend ourselves and the whole creation to your
   unfailing love.

Merciful Father . . .

This is the simplest way to start adapting the basic framework to the specific needs of a particular situation, bringing in the news of the day and the needs of the community. Next we look at a second way of using this time-honoured template.

5

Using the basic pattern (2)

The second option with the basic template is to integrate the specific petitions suitable for the occasion into the prayers, again using a response to help break things up and enable both silence and participation. In the example below, the words have been added before, in the middle, or at the end of each section, as you will see. It is important to note that sometimes the wording of the original will need altering slightly to make this work. The additions in the prayers below are indicated by italics. In this case the pattern is:

¶ Prayer
¶ Short silence
¶ Response.

A fully worked out example

In the power of the Spirit and in union with Christ,
let us pray to the Father.

Almighty God, our heavenly Father,
you promised through your Son Jesus Christ
to hear us when we pray in faith.

May your blessing be on Archbishop Rowan and Pope Benedict as they meet together.
Strengthen *N* our bishop and all your Church in the service of Christ. *Enrich the faith of the people of Berlin and all those celebrating the Kirchentag, and guide all* those who confess your name *to* be united in your truth, live together in your love, and reveal your glory in the world.

Short silence

Lord, in your mercy
hear our prayer.

Bless and guide Elizabeth our Queen;
give wisdom to all in authority;
and direct this and every nation in the ways of justice and of peace;
that we may honour one another, and seek the common good.
We ask your blessing especially on all those working for peace in the
Middle East,
and those engaged in rebuilding a just and peaceful society in Iraq.
Give your strength and courage to all those who live their lives
in the shadow of tyranny and oppression.

Short silence

Lord, in your mercy
hear our prayer.

We pray for all those returning to education after the summer holidays,
especially the staff of St James's school, and for its place in our
community.
Give grace to us, our families and friends, and to all our neighbours,
that we may serve Christ in one another, and love as he loves us.

Short silence

Lord, in your mercy
hear our prayer.

Comfort and heal all those who suffer in body, mind, or spirit,
especially . . . (a list of names follows) . . .
and all those being cared for in the nursing homes of this parish.
Give them courage and hope in their troubles;
and bring them the joy of your salvation.

Short silence

Lord, in your mercy
hear our prayer.

Hear us as we remember those who have died in the faith
of Christ.
We remember Jane Smith,
and all those whose year's mind[5] falls at this time, especially John Brown.
We thank you for the ways in which you brightened our lives by their
faith and friendship.

According to your promises,
grant us with them a share in your
eternal kingdom.

Short silence

Lord, in your mercy
hear our prayer.

In silence let us offer our own prayers to our heavenly Father.

Short silence

Rejoicing in the fellowship of *the Blessed Virgin Mary* and
all your saints,
we commend ourselves and the whole creation to your
unfailing love.

Merciful Father . . .

The types of alteration in the prayer for the world, where everything comes after the standard words, or the prayer for the local community, where everything comes before the standard words, are the easiest ways to combine your own words with the provided template. The first petition, however, for the Church, shows that it can be more complicated. The first phrase has become a complete sentence, ending in '. . . service of Christ'. Then the prayer replaces the link word 'that' with a whole new phrase: 'Enrich the faith of the people of Berlin and all those celebrating the *Kirchentag*, and guide . . .'. Finally, it is important to note the last change, which is the apparently minor, and easily overlooked, need to replace the word 'may' with the word 'to'. This change is needed because the *Kirchentag* petition has altered the grammar of the sentence, as well as adding new words.

The best way of catching this kind of problem is to read your prayers aloud as part of your preparation. You will not only spot this kind of potential problem more easily, but you will also discover if you have inadvertently slipped a tongue-twister into your prayers. Remember that the prayers are spoken language that just happens to be written down in preparation. Reading them aloud helps check whether what you have written is easy to say. As we take the pattern further in the following sections, and move further towards freshly written prayers, this becomes even more important.

6

Taking the pattern further

At this point it is worth remembering that the pattern discussed in previous chapters is just that: a template. The same words do not have to be used from week to week. Instead, the words printed in *Common Worship*, that we have been looking at, provide a worked out example of using the template pattern. But within this pattern we have the flexibility to use completely different words.

Here is a further example, sticking to the pattern and reusing the same special topics, but with completely different wording.

In your own words

In the power of the Spirit and in union with Christ,
let us pray to the Father.

Gracious God,
you delight to hear the prayers of your children,
and by your Spirit you help us to pray.

Hear us as we seek your blessing on the Archbishop of Canterbury, that his meeting with Pope Benedict may be fruitful for all your Church. Guide *N* our bishop with your wisdom, that he may lead us in the way of Christ. Enrich our partners in Berlin through their *Kirchentag*, and strengthen the bonds between us. Through sharing worship and joining together in your mission, may we know and serve Christ more faithfully.

Short silence

Lord, in your mercy
hear our prayer.

Teach the leaders of the nations to hunger and thirst for justice, and work tirelessly for peace. Encourage all those working for new ways forward in the Middle East, and strengthen those engaged in the rebuilding of Iraq. Be with all who live under tyrannous and oppressive governments, and help them to find the freedom that leads to peace.

Short silence

Lord, in your mercy
hear our prayer.

We give you thanks for all those who teach in our schools, and pray for them and all staff and pupils starting a new term. We hold before you the life of St James's school in this community. May all our schools be places where truth is sought and taught, and where everyone learns the value of mutual respect.

Short silence

Lord, in your mercy
hear our prayer.

We hold in your presence all who receive care in the nursing homes of this parish, and thank you for the care and dedication of the staff. We name before you all those with particular needs who have asked for our prayers, especially . . . *(a list of names follows).* May they know your presence with them, and that you are their strength, their healing, and their salvation.

Short silence

Lord, in your mercy
hear our prayer.

We give you thanks for all those who have brightened our lives by their faith and friendship, and entrust our sister Jane Smith into your hands. We remember John Brown and all those whose year's mind falls at this time. May we with them come to the fullness of joy in your eternal presence.

Short silence

Lord, in your mercy
hear our prayer.

In silence let us offer our own prayers to our heavenly Father.

Short silence

> We rejoice in the fellowship we share with the Blessed Virgin Mary
> and all your saints. Encouraged by this great cloud of witnesses,
> may we follow in the footsteps of Christ, and come at last to our
> eternal home.
>
> Merciful Father . . .

Some of the phrases here draw on the praying tradition of the Church.
Take 'year's mind', for example – this is a way of referring to the
anniversary of someone's death. Other phrases draw on familiar words
from Scripture, such as 'hunger and thirst for justice' (cf. Matthew 5.6)
or 'great cloud of witnesses' (Hebrews 12.1). Even when prayers are
written afresh, the language can draw on a wide range of traditional
ideas and phrases. In fact, of the two Scripture references just
mentioned, the first is a metaphor still understandable to people who
have not heard the Beatitudes (Matthew 5.1–12). The second probably
doesn't make as much sense to someone unfamiliar with that passage
from the Letter to the Hebrews. It is worth thinking about the use
(or overuse) of scriptural and traditional phrases in relation to the
specific congregation you will be leading in prayer. Will using sources
like these enrich the prayers, or will they cause confusion or distract
people from what you are saying?

In workshops I have led, there is a point when some people start to
wonder if progressing much further beyond the basic pattern will
simply become too complex. However, in all sorts of ways it sounds
much harder in theory than it is in practice. Many people, when
learning to drive, think they will never remember all the actions that
need to be co-ordinated to start the car up and move off when on a hill.
Steering wheel, clutch, accelerator and hand-brake engage each foot
and hand simultaneously. Nevertheless, nearly anyone can and does
learn to do it in the end. Leading prayer may seem to include too much
to remember at the same time, but, just as with a hill-start, it can
quickly become second nature. As we move on to further variations,
it's helpful to bear that in mind!

7

Variations on the pattern

Simply because there are five main sections in the template does not mean that we are always confined to five petitions. Sometimes, particularly in the light of a major event, a tragedy, or a crisis, or simply because we are inspired by a significant moment, we will want to insert an extra petition focusing on that specific topic.

For example, on the arrival in the diocese of a new bishop, we may want to add a separate petition. This will still form part of the first section, *praying for the Church*, but it will stand separately from a more general prayer on that theme. At the time of a general election, we may want to add a second petition to the section on the world. A first prayer for the world might focus on the national situation while a second takes up concerns elsewhere in the world. These are just two illustrations of how we might respond to particular circumstances.

Equally, we might decide to break most sections up into two or more shorter petitions, each followed by a response. When we do this there is less need for silence. What works instead is a reasonable pause after each petition and response. Here is another worked example, this time with shorter petitions, and a different response, but again covering exactly the same topics as we have used before.

An example with shorter petitions

In the power of the Spirit and in union with Christ,
let us pray to the Father.

Heavenly Father,
pour out your Spirit on your Church,
that following Jesus we may learn to pray:

Your kingdom come:
your will be done.

Bless *N* our archbishop, *N* our bishop, and all whom you have called

to ministry in your Church with the gifts of your Spirit, that they
may help us follow Christ more faithfully.

Your kingdom come:
your will be done.

We pray for the meeting of Archbishop Rowan and Pope Benedict.
We remember our partners in Berlin and all those sharing in their
Kirchentag with them. Build up the unity of your Church.

Your kingdom come:
your will be done.

Give wisdom and encouragement to all those working for peace in
the Middle East, and may peacemakers everywhere know the
blessing of being your children.

Your kingdom come:
your will be done.

May all those struggling for justice in the face of tyranny and
violence have the courage and strength to continue to seek for
justice, and hold to what is right.

Your kingdom come:
your will be done.

You are a God who delights in truth. Instil in all those engaged in
teaching and learning in our schools and colleges a love of what is
good and true.

Your kingdom come:
your will be done.

We thank you for the work of those in the nursing and residential
homes of this parish. Refresh them with your energy and
compassion, that they may minister your love to those in
their care.

Your kingdom come:
your will be done.

We hold before you all those in need of care and healing . . .

[especially] . . . *(names may be added, or a pause left)* . . . May they
know your healing and loving presence.

Your kingdom come:
your will be done.

We remember with thanksgiving Jane Smith, and all who have
recently died. We thank you also for John Brown, and all whose
anniversaries of death fall at this time. Bring us with all the faithful
departed to the fullness of joy in your presence.

Your kingdom come:
your will be done.

Rejoicing in the fellowship of the Blessed Virgin Mary,
    St James, and all your saints,
we commend ourselves and the whole creation to your
    unfailing love.

Merciful Father . . .

In this variation, the pattern is essentially the same, using the
same basic template of:

¶ the Church
¶ the world
¶ the local community
¶ those in need
¶ those who have died.

What is different is the pacing, which is more responsive and less
reflective. A greater number of shorter petitions can sometimes be
more engaging, especially when there are people present who are
relatively unused to following longer prayers, or using silence. It is
important to keep an eye on the length of petitions. You should
avoid adding more petitions, all of which are lengthy and better
suited to the more reflective style.

8

An alternative pattern

Dividing up topics for prayer into five main subject areas is the most common and familiar pattern. However, it is not the only template, although it does have the advantage of clarifying for everyone exactly where they are going, and what they will be praying for. There are, however, other possibilities that may be used. One other pattern from our tradition is essentially threefold:

¶ the world
¶ the Church
¶ individuals in need.

The Anglican use of this pattern is based on a frequently used prayer from the 1662 *Book of Common Prayer*: 'A Collect or Prayer for All Sorts and Conditions of Men'.[6] This seems to have originally been intended as a summary or catch-all prayer to stand in for the many and various petitions of the litany on occasions when the latter was not used.

A threefold pattern

In the power of the Spirit and in union with Christ,
let us pray to the Father.

O God, the creator and preserver of all,
we pray for people in every kind of need;
make your ways known on earth,
your saving health among all nations . . .
(particular petitions may be added)

Silence may be kept

A short response may be used

We pray for the good estate of the catholic Church;
guide and govern us by your good Spirit,
that all who profess and call themselves Christians
may be led into the way of truth,

and hold the faith in unity of spirit,
in the bond of peace and in righteousness of life . . .
(particular petitions may be added)

Silence may be kept

A short response may be used

We commend to your fatherly goodness
all those who are any ways afflicted or distressed,
in mind, body or estate;
comfort and relieve them in their need,
give them patience in their sufferings,
and bring good out of all their afflictions . . .
(particular petitions may be added)

Silence may be kept

A short response may be used

We remember those who have gone before us
in the peace of Christ,
and we give you praise for all your faithful ones,
with whom we rejoice in the communion of saints . . .
(names may be added)

All this we ask for Jesus Christ's sake.
Amen.

The eagle-eyed reader will have counted the paragraphs here and
wondered whether this is in fact a fourfold pattern. In *Common
Worship*,[7] the original prayer has had *a remembrance of those who
have died* added to it. In terms of the template, however, this is better
seen either as an expansion of the section praying for those in
particular need, or as a way of concluding the whole. Sticking with the
original pattern, a simple threefold template of world, Church and
individuals offers a better contrast with the more common fivefold
pattern, and is a more helpful shorter form.

This simpler form may sometimes be more appropriate when brevity
is called for: on weekdays, or in residential care homes. However, a
template of three main sections may also be useful on other occasions
– for example, with the use of prayer chants like those from Taizé. (See
page 38.) It can be used in the same variety of ways as the basic fivefold
pattern, and adapted just as in the various examples above. So it is

possible to develop it by adding simple statements (as in Chapter 4), or by inserting additional text (as in Chapter 5). Likewise, prayers can be rewritten (as in Chapter 6) or expanded into several shorter petitions (as in Chapter 7). The same principles apply to both the fivefold and threefold templates. As we move on to some other ways of leading prayer, we will also learn some additional principles.

9

A different style of prayer: biddings

The words we have looked at so far, and the different ways they can be used, have been patterns of *prayers*. In other words, they have been addressed directly to God. There is, however, an alternative style, called *biddings*, in which the congregation is invited to pray, and the congregational praying comes in the silence and response. You may be most familiar with this idea from the bidding prayer[8] that often begins a carol service, lists some things to be prayed for, and then concludes by inviting everyone to pray for them by saying the Lord's Prayer.

When this style of bidding is used for the intercessions, it usually consists of very brief biddings, and the congregation then prays using a short prayer response. There is usually a short pause, or a longer and more reflective space for silent prayer. Each bidding is an *invitation* to pray; each congregational response is the actual prayer. The bidding usually ends with words such as: 'let us pray to the Lord'. The actual prayer is the response that follows: 'Lord, have mercy' – one of the most ancient prayer responses used by the Church.

When using this pattern it is very important to remember that God is not addressed directly, except in the response. It is the congregation that is addressed directly: you are asking them to pray. So it is, for example, 'his Church' and not 'your Church'. The words 'you' and 'your' always refer to the congregation that is being invited to say their prayers. Here is an example from *Common Worship*.[9]

Bidding prayers

> In the power of the Spirit and in union with Christ,
> let us pray to the Father.

For the peace of the whole world,
for the welfare of the Holy Church of God,
and for the unity of all,
let us pray to the Lord.
Lord, have mercy.

For *N* our bishop,
for the leaders of our sister Churches,
and for all clergy and people,
let us pray to the Lord.
Lord, have mercy.

For *Elizabeth our Queen*,
for the leaders of the nations,
and for all in authority,
let us pray to the Lord.
Lord, have mercy.

For this community,
for every city, town and village,
and for all the people who live within them,
let us pray to the Lord.
Lord, have mercy.

For good weather,
and for abundant harvests for all to share,
let us pray to the Lord.
Lord, have mercy.

For those who travel by land, air, or water,
for the sick and the suffering,
[for . . .,]
for prisoners and captives,
and for their safety, health and salvation,
let us pray to the Lord.
Lord, have mercy.

For our deliverance from all affliction, strife and need,
and for the absolution of our sins and offences,
let us pray to the Lord.
Lord, have mercy.

Remembering [. . . and]
all who have gone before us in faith,
and in communion with [. . . and] all the saints,
we commit ourselves, one another,
and our whole life to the Lord our God.

Silence may be kept and a collect or other ending may be said

This is nowadays the most common form of bidding. In the next section, however, we will look at another one, which is deeply rooted in past tradition.

10

A different style of prayer: biddings with collects

One of the ways of praying that has been most characteristic of the Anglican heritage is the use of biddings combined with collects. When the church used the 1662 *Book of Common Prayer* exclusively, there was no flexibility in the words of the prayers at Holy Communion. The only place where people had some flexibility in leading prayer was at Matins and Evensong. When the first generations of lay people began to lead prayer in church, these services provided the pattern they learnt to follow.

As a matter of fact, they drew on an older style of prayer, which can still be seen in the principal liturgy for Good Friday, one of the few places it has survived outside cathedral Evensong. Here is just a short excerpt from these solemn prayers of Good Friday.[10]

> Let us pray for the nations of the world and their leaders:
> for Elizabeth our Queen and the Parliaments of this land
> for those who administer the law and all who serve in public office,
> for all who strive for justice and reconciliation,
> that by God's help the world may live in peace and freedom.

> *Silence is kept*

> Lord, hear us.
> **Lord, graciously hear us.**

> Most gracious God and Father,
> in whose will is our peace,
> turn our hearts and the hearts of all to yourself,
> that by the power of your Spirit
> the peace which is founded on justice
> may be established throughout the world;
> through Jesus Christ our Lord.
> **Amen.**

This follows the same template throughout the prayers. More generally, and not just on Good Friday, this pattern can be represented like this:

¶ Bidding   'Let us pray for . . . that . . .'

¶ Silence   This is more substantial than that in the more common patterns.

¶ Response   This may be omitted at, say, Evensong, and its function replaced by the collect's 'Amen'.

¶ Collect   A suitable collect that picks up the topic of the bidding.

Prayers following this template include more words and more silence than the patterns to which we have become accustomed. When collects are used, for example, in cathedral Evensong, they tend to have shorter biddings than the Good Friday prayers and are usually used without a response. It may be that on occasion (perhaps particularly at Evensong) it is right to draw on this particular pattern, with its (very Anglican) devotion to collect-style prayers. It is a variation of the bidding template that follows the same rules, except that, as well as or instead of a response, it finishes each section with a collect.

11

Using the alternative pattern of biddings

The alternative pattern just described can be used exactly as printed in Chapter 9 (p. 23), adding the particular names and situations to be prayed for. It can also be adapted just as easily and variously as the basic fivefold and threefold patterns we have already looked at. It is usually best if the invitations to pray are relatively brief. There can be more of them for each topic, as in Chapter 7 (p. 17). In the example that follows, note that the prayers overall follow exactly the same order as the fivefold pattern: Church, world, community, those in need, the communion of saints. Note also that we are using exactly the same situations and topics as we have used in the earlier examples.

Adapting the bidding model

In the power of the Spirit and in union with Christ,
let us pray to the Father.

For Rowan, Archbishop of Canterbury, and his meeting with
    Pope Benedict,
and for our partners in Berlin and their *Kirchentag*,
that God may deepen the Church's unity,
let us pray to the Lord.
Lord, have mercy.

For N our bishop,
and the life of this diocese,
that we may follow Christ more faithfully,
let us pray to the Lord.
Lord, have mercy.

For the peoples of the Middle East,
that God will bless them with peace,

let us pray to the Lord.
Lord, have mercy.

For all who struggle against tyranny
and the threat of violence,
that God will guide their search for justice,
let us pray to the Lord.
Lord, have mercy.

For all in our schools: staff and students,
that God will grant them his wisdom,
and give them a love of truth,
let us pray to the Lord.
Lord, have mercy.

For the residential care homes of this parish,
that God may fill all who work in them with strength
    and compassion,
and keep all who live in them secure in love,
let us pray to the Lord.
Lord, have mercy.

For all those in need,
[especially . . .]
that God may surround them with his healing love,
let us pray to the Lord.
Lord, have mercy.

For [N and] all our brothers and sisters
who have gone to their rest in the hope of rising again,
that God will shine the light of the resurrection on them,
let us pray to the Lord.
Lord, have mercy.

In silence let us offer our own prayers to our heavenly Father.

Silence may be kept and a collect or other ending may be said.

In the last three chapters we have looked at the fundamental style of using biddings to pray. In the next chapter we need to look briefly at the details of the language we use to do it.

12

On the vocabulary of biddings

With the bidding pattern there is a typical 'grammar', which I have used in full in the prayers in Chapter 11. Very broadly speaking, people and situations to pray for are introduced by the word 'for'. In fact, each bidding in this example begins like that. Equally typically, the things we are asking for are introduced by the word 'that'. Again, in this example each bidding asks for something 'that' God will do. This gives a pattern where we pray 'for X, that God will do Y'.

This is not set in stone, but it can help keep our thinking and praying clear. It is possible simply to mention the people or situations we are praying for, and not ask anything specific, as in the *Common Worship* example in Chapter 9 (p. 23):

> For this community,
> for every city, town and village,
> and for all the people who live within them,
> let us pray to the Lord.
> **Lord, have mercy.**

It is also possible to introduce some of the things we are praying for with the word 'for' – it is by far the most common word to start a bidding. Again the *Common Worship* template in Chapter 9 provides an example, as in this petition:

> For good weather,
> and for abundant harvests for all to share,
> let us pray to the Lord.
> **Lord, have mercy.**

It is also possible, though less common, to begin a bidding simply with 'that' so that the person or situation being prayed for is implicit in the prayer. This tends to result in shorter litanies, for example:

> That God will bring justice to his world,
> let us pray to the Lord.
> **Lord, have mercy.**
>
> That God will bring peace between nations,
> let us pray to the Lord.
> **Lord, have mercy.**

There is, in short, no single way to structure a bidding; only a range of typical ways such as those illustrated here. The style is, however, sufficiently different from the more common one of direct prayers to make it worth paying careful attention to the language until you get used to it.

The *main* language point to watch out for, however, is to be very careful about not saying 'you' and 'your' when that would refer to God. In biddings, the leader is addressing the congregation, and the congregation with the leader addresses God in the response. I don't think it would be too much to express this as a rule for leading this style of prayer: look at every instance of the words 'you' and 'your' in the prayers and ask yourself whether it means God (in which case change it) or the congregation, and in that case, it would probably be more natural to say 'us' and 'our'.

From this very specific examination of the ways of leading prayers with biddings, we return to more general points about the whole range of ways to lead prayer, beginning with the use of responses.

13

Thinking about responses

Most of the forms of prayer we use, and all those that we have looked at so far in this booklet, use responses. The two most commonly used responses are:

> Lord, in your mercy
> **hear our prayer.**

and

> Lord, hear us.
> **Lord, graciously hear us.**

These should, over time, become so much second nature that people do not need to be told them, just as we know automatically to say 'Amen' at the end of a collect. It's good for congregations to become familiar with joining in the prayers in this way, and only when there are numbers of visitors present should people need to be told what these responses are.

Announcing the response

When people do need to be told the response, either because of a significant number of new people or because an unfamiliar one is being used, it is best to explain clearly and concisely, and give the congregation a chance to say the response immediately. Here is one simple form of explanatory wording that can be used right at the beginning of the intercessions:

> There is a short response to each of these prayers. After the words 'Father, by your Spirit', will you please respond 'bring in your kingdom'?
>
> **In the power of the Spirit and in union with Christ,**
> **let us pray to the Father.**

> Father, by your Spirit
> **bring in your kingdom.**

Or, very similarly, you might say:

> There is a short response to each of these prayers. The response
> to the words 'Father, by your Spirit' is 'bring in your kingdom'.
>
> In the power of the Spirit and in union with Christ,
> let us pray to the Father.
>
> Father, by your Spirit
> **bring in your kingdom.**

Some people choose to do a rehearsal straight after telling the
congregation what the response is, like this:

> There is a short response to each of these prayers. After the
> words 'Father, by your Spirit', please respond 'bring in your
> kingdom'.
>
> Father, by your Spirit
> **bring in your kingdom.**

You will know what works best in your congregation. However, the
advantage to the first two ways of doing it is that it is then actually the
first prayer of the prayers, rather than a practice run.

A range of responses

There is a range of short responses that may sometimes be chosen for a
particular reason. We have seen the following so far:

> Lord, in your mercy
> **hear our prayer.**
>
> Lord, hear us.
> **Lord, graciously hear us.**
>
> Father, by your Spirit
> **bring in your kingdom.**
>
> Your kingdom come.
> **your will be done.**

These are all straightforward, and use simple phrases, often familiar ones. They are all appropriate for either of the two basic patterns. There are other good simple responses that you can use for the basic pattern, including:

> Faithful God
> **glorify your name.**

> Lord of love and mercy
> **hear our prayer.**

> Father of all
> **hear your children's prayer.**

> . . . we pray to you, O Lord.
> **Lord, have mercy.**

Many other examples can be found. Existing responses can also be adapted. For example, in the following example:

> Lord of love and mercy
> **hear our prayer.**

'Lord of love and mercy' can easily be altered to fit the occasion or the topic; for example:

> Lord of compassion . . .
> Lord of heaven and earth . . .
> Lord of glory . . .
> Lord of creation . . .

The list of possible variations is not quite endless, but it's certainly lengthy.

All these responses share the merits of being short and easily remembered. Among other resources for further examples, *New Patterns for Worship*[11] is particularly helpful.

The alternative style and its response

The alternative style has its own typical response, equally short and easily remembered, as we have already seen:

> . . . let us pray to the Lord.
> **Lord, have mercy.**

The styles for the basic pattern, and this simple response to the alternative pattern, do not lend themselves to mixing and matching. Keep this last response for the alternative style, but use any of the other types of responses for the basic patterns. This is also a reminder that problems can arise through picking the wrong response, and we need to look at some of those problems next.

14

Problems with responses

Problems with responses come in several varieties, depending on the type of response and how it fits into the pattern. There are some responses that pose particular problems. Take a look at this one:

> Jesus, Lord of life,
> **in your mercy, hear us.**

It is short, and it is memorable, but it is addressed to Jesus. While most of the time our intercessions are addressed to God the Father, there is absolutely nothing wrong with choosing a more thematic set addressed to Jesus (for example, at Christmas or Easter).[12]

If you use a response addressed to Jesus, however, you need to take special care to make sure that the prayers themselves are addressed to Jesus as well. Consistency is very important, and choosing this response may mean extra work has to be put into the prayers.

Another sort of response has different problems. One, for example, that has sometimes been used in churches where I have worshipped, is this one:

> God our Father
> **let your will be done in us.**

(There are other, similar types of response around.) There will be some sets of prayers for which this response might be appropriate. However, if we are praying for an archbishop, or for leaders of countries involved in peace talks (to give two examples), is it really appropriate to pray 'let your will be done in us'? After all, the body of the prayer is a prayer for *them*, not for *us*. It is better if the response is also a prayer for them, or more generally for everyone. As a rule, to which there are always exceptions, our prayers of intercession are concerned with others more than ourselves. It can help if the response doesn't draw the focus back to us all the time, but keeps it on those others for whom we are praying. A better response might be:

> God our Father
> **let your will be done.**

Simply omitting the words 'in us' allows the focus of the response to remain on those for whom we are praying, while still keeping the central thrust of the response on God's will.

Other responses are not particularly helpful because they are too long or complicated; for example:

> Come in mercy, Lord
> **and bathe our world in the light of your wonderful love.**

Before the congregation gets to the first time this is used after a prayer, some will be thinking it began 'and' and others 'bathe'. Others will remember the whole phrase, while some will shorten it mentally to 'light of your love'. Any response this long will normally encourage people to make mistakes.

The standard advice is well worth bearing in mind: 'Keep it short and simple.' The shorter something is, the more easily remembered it is. This matters, since the whole point of the response is to enable people to articulate the fact that these are *their* prayers, and not just *your* prayers.

The one possible exception to keeping it simple can be when a musical response is being used, and it is to sung responses that we turn next.

15

Singing the responses

Singing responses can introduce a different style of participation, because it engages more parts of our self than words on their own do. Something of this idea is expressed in a maxim regularly attributed to St Augustine: 'The one who sings prays twice.'[13] Music can reach where words do not. It is also a feature of sung responses that, while often quite simple, people can also cope with sung responses that are more complicated since the tune is an aid to remembering the words. Sung responses can also engage people who have problems with words in general. I learned that lesson when a child with learning difficulties started attending church regularly with her family. The first part of the service she was able to join in was neither a simple response nor a children's song. It was the *Gloria*, sung regularly to the same setting, and in the part of the service before the children left for their own instruction. Singing should not be underestimated as a means of participation for those excluded by words and complex meanings. On some occasions it can be quite appropriate to use a sung response.

Using Taizé chants

Some of the most common forms of prayer chant are those that have entered church life through the community at Taizé. The alternative style of prayer, because it is rooted in the traditions of a sung litany, has often had a sung response, such as this one from Taizé:

> Kyrie, kyrie eleison.

This is simply the Greek (the language of the early Church and the New Testament) for 'Lord, Lord, have mercy'. If you are using a response like this, then either everyone can sing it after the words 'Let us pray to the Lord' or a cantor can sing it after those words and then everyone can repeat it.

Other forms of sung response may work better with the shorter threefold basic pattern instead of the longer fivefold one. Again, one or more of the chants from the Taizé community are often used, like

'O Lord, hear my prayer' or 'Jesus, remember me'. (Books of Taizé prayers and songs are readily available. They are also printed in some hymnbooks. If you need help learning the chants, you can download individual songs from the *iTunes*™ store and other sources of digital music.)

New Patterns for Worship includes several sung responses:[14]

> O Lord, hear my prayer (Taizé)
> Through our lives and by our prayers (Iona)
> Oculi nostri / Our eyes are opened (Taizé)
> Watch, watch and pray (Iona)
> Jesus Christ, Son of God (Iona)

Music from these two very different communities is a resource that can enrich the praying life of many churches. Their repertoires, however, are starting places rather than denoting the limits of what can be used.

Quite often, in these situations, repeating each sung response at least two or three times both creates a prayerful mood and helps people reflect on what they are praying for. Some responses (such as the Taizé Kyrie mentioned above) lend themselves to being sung once in response to a bidding, while others ('O Lord, hear my prayer', for example) lend themselves well to being sung several times as part of a reflective response.

Two things must be said about this use of repetitive sung responses. Generally they will work best when there are few topics of prayer being covered – so, for example, with the threefold pattern rather than with the fivefold one. It is also the case that the more reflective style they engender will not be best suited to the pacing of a regular and typical parish Eucharist, but to more occasional use. They can lend themselves to accompanying activity in all-age worship (see page 44) or they can work well in evening worship when there is often less time pressure.

As with any new piece of music, it is very helpful to have a group of singers who are well-practised – this does not need to be a traditional choir, although it may very well be one – not only to help lead the chant, but also to teach new chants or sung responses to the congregation before the act of worship begins.

Adapting other songs

You can also choose to adapt appropriate choruses or songs. Take, for example, the well-known chorus, 'Spirit of the living God, fall afresh on me'.[15] This can be adapted by singing, depending on the topic of the petition, '. . . fall afresh on them' and '. . . fall afresh on us'.

Or there is the even better known 'Kum-ba-yah'. Because of its use in many primary school assemblies this can often be a particularly helpful one to adapt on certain occasions when there may be numbers of children unused to church present for some particular gathering. Obviously the regularly used verse is appropriate:

> Someone's praying Lord, kum-ba-yah,
> Someone's praying Lord, kum-ba-yah,
> Someone's praying Lord, kum-ba-yah,
> Oh, Lord, kum-ba-yah.

It can equally be adapted to be more specific to what is being prayed for. 'Someone's fighting, Lord . . .' and 'Someone's hurting, Lord . . .' are just two examples. None of these require any great level of musical skill, but often sung responses of this sort enable a different kind of participation than a said one does.

It is possible, also, to interleave prayers with songs and hymns. Again, this is probably best done only on particular occasions, and in circumstances when a far more meditative style of prayer is desirable or appropriate. One of the things to avoid in this is overly frequent novelty, instead aiming to help congregations inhabit some regular patterns with which they are 'at home'. Then the occasional visit to another style of 'house' can be enriching and rewarding, rather than off-putting. Two examples of this might be to lead reflective prayers on the cross in our world alternating with verses of the traditional hymn 'The royal banners forward go',[16] or prayers for justice and peace interwoven with verses of the contemporary song 'Beauty for brokenness'.[17] I include a worked example in Appendix C.

There are some additional practicalities that you need to be aware of when using music in this way. The first is copyright. Most songs are covered by one or other of two licensing schemes. The larger scheme is administered by Christian Copyright Licensing International (CCLI) whose web site is http://www.ccli.co.uk. This issues a variety of licences, at fees varying according to the size of your congregation, and beginning with a basic licence to print the words on service sheets or project them onto a screen. It covers a very wide range of music, including most new songs emerging out of evangelical and renewal circles. It also covers the chants referred to above published by the Wild Goose Resource Group. The other main scheme, Calamus, is administered by Decani Music (http://www.decanimusic.co.uk). The cost of this licence scheme is also based on the size of the congregation, but includes the printing/projection of a melody line with the words. It covers the music of the Taizé community and a range of liturgical music and contemporary songs used particularly (but by no means exclusively) in Roman Catholic circles. These schemes provide a relatively low-cost way of widening a church's repertoire of music by allowing local printing or digital projection, and many churches make use of them both.

It is worth keeping an ear open for musical items in your church's repertoire that could lend themselves to this kind of adaptation. Before looking at other ways of developing participation in Chapter 17, we need to look at a very particular sort of response: how we bring the prayers to an end.

16

Beginnings and endings for prayer

The beginnings and endings of the intercessions are two of those points in an act of worship when I am reminded that there is no such thing as 'normal' in the Church of England. In some churches the president tops and tails the prayers with the invitation to pray, and a collect or other ending (such as those printed on pages 288–9 of the *Common Worship* main volume). In other churches a lay leader of prayer does everything, and in others again there is an expectation that the president will invite people to pray, while the lay leader of the prayers leads the ending. Ultimately, the most important thing is to be very clear about who is doing what. It is not good practice, for example, for the president to signal the start of the prayers with words such as 'In the power of the Spirit, and in union with Christ, let us pray to the Father' and then the leader of the intercessions to say, 'Let us pray for the Church and for the world, and let us thank God for his goodness.' After being invited to pray, we should pray, not get invited to do so all over again.

Liturgical purists would argue that the model of presidency adopted in *Common Worship* is of having a single minister preside over the whole of the act of worship with a particular responsibility to ensure it all coheres into a single whole. This model suggests that the presider is the best person to top and tail the prayers, and weave them into the fabric of the whole act of worship. This approach certainly has something to commend it, and can, at a pragmatic level, provide a helpful and experienced safety net for the person leading the prayers. However, being purist is less important than being clear. The presider needs to know what the leader of the intercessions is going to do, and vice versa. Confusion is not helpful – either to those involved in leading, or to those being led in prayer.

The most common ending used by those who lead intercessions is that borrowed from the basic pattern, or a similar form of words:

Rejoicing in the fellowship of [N and of] all your saints,
we commend ourselves and the whole creation to your
   unfailing love.

Merciful Father
accept these prayers
for the sake of your Son
our Saviour Jesus Christ. Amen.

A collect provided in *Common Worship* which is becoming quite
widely used is this one:[18]

Almighty God,
by your Holy Spirit you have made us one
with your saints in heaven and on earth:
grant that in our earthly pilgrimage
we may ever be supported by this fellowship of love and prayer,
and know ourselves surrounded by their witness to your power
   and mercy;
through Jesus Christ our Lord.
Amen.

Both these have in common not only a general 'wrapping up' feel to
them, but a reminder that we are part of a fellowship of prayer that
spans the ages, and is alive in God's eternal presence. This makes a
fitting conclusion, and can, of course, as an idea, be adapted
appropriately as the other prayers can be. For a selection of further
appropriate endings, see the above-mentioned pages 288–9 of
Common Worship: Services and Prayers for the Church of England and
some further ones in *New Patterns for Worship* on pages 181–2.

What is most important, irrespective of any particular beginning
and ending, is that it should be obvious that the prayers have begun
and ended. At the Eucharist a clear ending will normally indicate to
the congregation that it is the right time to prepare for the Peace. On
all occasions it will help people move to the next part of the worship
with confidence.

In the previous chapter we were beginning to explore, with the help
of music, some of the ways to develop the prayers further beyond being
simply a template of words. Next we will look at some different
methods for taking things further.

17

Taking it further: greater spoken participation

In looking at developing the prayers of our congregations, one of the simplest ways is to involve more people. Although the traditional model features a single leader of the prayers, there is no need for this always to be the case. In situations where the prayers are not led by a single person, it helps, as suggested above, to have the president introduce and conclude the prayers.

Consider trying the following. With prayers consisting of short petitions, try two leaders – one woman (A) and one man (B), or one adult (A) and one child (B) – alternating the petitions between them. Here is a simple excerpted example:

A   Give grace to us, our families and friends, and to all our neighbours, that we may serve Christ in one another, and love as he loves us.

      Short silence

      Lord, in your mercy
All   **hear our prayer**.

B   Comfort and heal all those who suffer in body, mind, or spirit . . .; give them courage and hope in their troubles; and bring them the joy of your salvation.

      Short silence

      Lord, in your mercy
All   **hear our prayer**.

Alternatively, it may be possible to involve a younger child, or a person (child or adult) with learning difficulties, in leading prayers, by asking them to lead the responses while one or more adults lead the main part of the prayers. In this case, the adult (A) leads the actual prayers with their more complicated and varied wording and the child or adult with learning difficulties (B) simply uses the familiar and simple response. The leading adult may need to give a signal (touching the shoulder perhaps) to help control the length of silence.

A   Give grace to us, our families and friends, and to all our neighbours, that we may serve Christ in one another, and love as he loves us.

Short silence

B   Lord, in your mercy
All   **hear our prayer.**

One of the important things about this is that it stresses our baptismal vocation to be involved as active pray-ers. Children are not simply consumers of activities staged for them by adults, but genuine participants able to help adults pray. Likewise, those with learning difficulties are members of the same body of Christ.

On another, perhaps most likely special, occasion with five main petitions, why not give one petition to each of five people spread around the congregation? They should all be encouraged to speak loudly and clearly. Each prayer should be numbered to ensure that the five people know which order they come in. (Alternatively, everyone can have a copy of all five, with their own petition highlighted.) Then the prayers are more audibly and visibly the prayers of the whole congregation. You will know whether your building (and/or technology) makes this a viable option.

In some congregations (particularly smaller ones) this can sometimes help lead to occasions when spoken congregational participation in the prayers is not limited to either responses or 'Amens', but can involve contributing biddings, or names spoken aloud, or, in the right context, their own prayers.

Increasing opportunities for more verbal participation is only one way forward. There are also ways of increasing active participation.

18

Taking it further: greater participation in action

There may be some occasions when it is appropriate to encourage action alongside or instead of the words of the prayers.

Research has repeatedly shown that different people have different ways of interacting with material. This research has been carried out in the realm of learning styles, but is also likely to be relevant to the ways we engage with worship and with words more generally. Some people do take in information primarily through the ear, while others are much more affected by the visual. Visual styles are not simply about projecting words and pictures onto a screen, but a whole thoughtful approach to the visual dynamics of the space where the congregation worships. It includes colour, sight-lines, and the location of the activity.

In addition to this research, increasing attention has been given to learning by participating in some form of action, or what are called kinaesthetic learning styles. Another way of thinking of these might be as *multi-sensory* forms of engagement with prayer and worship. In these approaches, the leadership comes much more in the preparation for these types of prayer than what is actually said on the day.

In the first two activities at least, you will find it helpful to have a series of Taizé chants or other short songs with prayerful words for people to join in while they participate in the activity.

Lighting candles

A great many people respond well to being invited to light a candle to symbolize their prayer. While the songs or chants are being sung (by everyone), invite people to come forward, light a candle and place it on one of the stands you have already prepared. These stands do not have to be elaborate. Candles can be placed safely on stone floors away from the main routes to and from doors and places such as the lectern or altar. They can also be placed in sand trays, either on the floor or on tables.

You will probably find it helpful to prime one or two individuals to start this, so that others can join in naturally and unselfconsciously.

Burning incense

An alternative to lighting candles is burning incense. Have a couple of well-insulated metal bowls or plates on either side of the altar table, or another appropriate place, with charcoal burning in them. Place beside them small bowls containing grains of incense. Invite people to come forward while the songs are being sung and take a grain or two of incense to represent their prayers, and place it on the lit charcoal. (Take care that the bowls are placed safely and securely.)

Particularly when children are involved in this activity, you may want to explain the simplest form of the symbolism: that the smoke represents our prayers going up to God, and the sweet smell of the incense represents the love with which he answers them coming down.

Prayer stations

This is a development of the above ideas, where people are invited to pray in several different ways. It might be particularly appropriate for an occasion where prayer is the main focus, and a congregation with a wide age range is present.

You can have prayer stations for lighting candles or burning incense as above. But you can add to them.

Perhaps add a map of the world pinned to a notice board. Invite people to stick a pin in the map for a country they want to pray for.

Or add one or two flip-charts around the church, and invite people to write on them the name of someone they want to pray for.

Provide a bowl of water and a pile of stones. Invite people to place a stone in the water for a sinful situation that needs God's cleansing forgiveness.

There is room for being creative in these or other ways that can sometimes help people to engage in prayer in new ways.

This is just a handful of ideas that seem to me to work well in a variety of situations. Some, such as the lighting of candles or burning of incense, I have found to be easily incorporated into a regular pattern of worship, and that they readily engage all ages. Others are much more likely to be successful when used on particular and special occasions. If this is something you want to start exploring or developing, then one of the better starting places is to be found in Scripture Union's 'Multi-sensory' series.[19]

The more adventurous you decide to be (and many of these ideas take up an indeterminate amount of time), the more important it becomes that you collaborate with the presider. For those who are wary of anything new, the sense that the presider (perhaps especially if it's the vicar) will be keeping an eye on things can really help to provide the impression of a safety net. In these circumstances the arguments for having the presider introduce and conclude the time of intercession become somewhat stronger.

19

Preparing yourself, preparing the prayers

Different people have different ways of preparing to lead the prayers. For those doing this for the first time, often it is simply a case of being familiar with one of the basic examples, and reading it well. But as you move on, you will want to start adapting other people's prayers or writing your own.

Five helpful tips

Let's start with the positive:

1. Build up a collection of phrases that you have heard in other people's prayers, or found helpful in books. Many of the phrases in the set versions go back a long way in the tradition of Christian prayers. Sometimes one will strike you as just right for one of your own prayers. When it comes to prayer, as in so many other things, we stand on the shoulders of giants, and can learn from the prayers of those who have gone before us. In doing this it becomes really useful to know your way around the content of the *Common Worship* material. In addition to *New Patterns for Worship, Common Worship: Daily Prayer*[20] is particularly useful here.

2. Look through the readings for the Sunday. They may suggest some obvious topics of prayer for you. If the Gospel reading is a story of Jesus healing the blind, it may be appropriate to include prayer for those with disabilities in your intercessions. There may be an emphasis on justice in a reading from the Prophets that you will want to echo, or a passage on unity from St Paul. Doing this also increases the chances that the sermon and the prayers will fit well together.

3. Make sure you know your church's system for handing in the names of those individuals to be prayed for. If there isn't one,

then perhaps you should organize one together. How will any individual be asked whether they want to be prayed for by name? Some people are very private about their problems, and will not want you broadcasting them, even with the best of intentions.

4. Keep an eye on the news in the days leading up to Sunday. Events taking place throughout the world will help you select the right topics to pray for. If possible, just before leaving the house for church, check the news on the radio, the television, or the Web. Something of major significance or a great tragedy may have happened overnight.

5. Let your public prayer grow out of your personal prayer. You will find ideas and phrases moving from one to the other. Don't try to pray like someone else, but remember that the intercessions are not simply your prayers, they are everyone else's prayers too. Something that can be quite appropriate in the quiet of your home may not be appropriate in the church.

Five things to watch out for

There are also some key things to avoid:

1. The prayers are not the notices. You really don't need to tell God when and where the Ladies' Group is meeting, or the time of Joe Bloggs's funeral.

2. The prayers are not a party political broadcast. 'We pray for the government, that it may be given wisdom to pursue God's justice in society' is acceptable and good practice. 'We pray for the government, that it will see common sense and bring back hanging and flogging' is not.

3. The prayers are not a sermon. From time to time we have all heard prayers that tell us what to think, prayers that are longer than the sermon, and prayers that have tried to correct the sermon. But the prayers are not you talking to people; they are you helping people talk to God.

4. The prayers are not everything. There are other opportunities in the service for praise and thanksgiving, for penitence and quiet, for belief and commitment to discipleship. You don't have to throw everything but the kitchen sink into the intercessions. Keep them focused, and then they will help

others focus on God and the people and situations being brought before him.

5.   The prayers need to be consistent. Don't mix 'thee/thou' language with 'you/your' language. Don't start by addressing the Father and end up addressing Jesus. Don't start by addressing God as 'you', and end up addressing the congregation as 'you'. Watch your language.

(If you want to engage in a fun way of reflecting on possible mistakes in prayers, either on your own or with a group, try the exercise in Appendix A.)

20

Sample intercessions

Any of the forms of prayer that we've looked at in the main part of the booklet can be used, or adapted. Here are six more sets of prayers that can act as intercessions to be used 'as is' when you're just beginning, adapted as you gain experience, or taken as templates for you to write your own as you develop your gifts. None of them is perfect and all of them can be improved by adaptation, but each is usable as it stands.

According to the basic fivefold pattern

All of these are intended to be used with silences and a short response between the petitions. Any appropriate ending may be used.

Sample set A

Let us pray for all God's good creation.

Gracious Lord, hear our prayers for your Church, together with N our archbishop and all whom you call to your service. Enable your Church in every place to witness to the good news of your love by its words and actions.

Give your wisdom to the leaders of every nation, that they may fulfil their calling and pursue justice and peace within and between countries. Guide the people of this land to be fair and generous in our public and private life together.

We seek your blessing on this community, our homes and our friends. Teach us to build up one another, and serve the needs of all.

We commend to your loving care all who are in need of healing. Give them patience and trust in your love. [Especially we pray for . . .] May they know the joy and wholeness your Son has come to bring.

We thank you for the lives of those whom we love but see no longer. Help us to trust them into your care, as we together wait for the resurrection and the restoration of all creation.

In silence let us offer our own prayers to our heavenly Father.

Sample set B

Let us pray for the Church and the world, and let us thank God for his goodness.

Heavenly Father, we thank you that you have called us into your Church, and entrusted us with your work in the world. Guide N our bishop, and all whom you have set over us, so that together we may deepen our knowledge of your truth, and share more widely the good news of your love.

You are a God who speaks in truth and love. Give wisdom and a love of truth to all who work in the media. Help them to discern what matters, draw attention to injustice, and promote greater understanding in our world.

We commend to you all who work, and especially those whose occupations seem menial and beneath notice. We thank you for the many invisible services that enrich our common life. Help us to value all who work in them, and treat them with respect and honour.

We hold in your presence all who are troubled and distressed, whether in body, mind or spirit. We remember all those who have asked for our prayers [, especially . . .]. May they know your presence with them, their strength, their encouragement, and their healing.

Remember, Lord, our brothers and sisters who have gone to their rest in the hope of rising again [, especially . . .]. May we with them enjoy the fullness of your presence.

In silence we bring our own prayers before God.

Sample set C

In the power of the Spirit and in union with Christ, let us pray to the Father.

Gracious and generous God, you enrich your Church with many good gifts. We thank you for our bishops and all who are called to the apostolic ministry. Help all your Church to live by the power of your Spirit, and use all that you have given us for the glory of your name and the good of all creation.

God of justice, you cast down those who overreach themselves in pride, and lift up the lowly. Give your blessing to all entrusted with power in our society, that they may exercise their authority in humility, and for the benefit of all. Teach us to build communities where all are valued.

God of self-sacrifice, we thank you for all who serve society in willing generosity. We pray for all who work in voluntary organizations, all who serve the needs of others, and all who devote themselves to caring for others. May they know the strength and encouragement of your example and companionship.

Healing God, we bring to you all those in need of care and compassion. Soothe the disordered mind, calm the troubled spirit, and ease the pains of the body. [Especially we pray for . . .] Fill them with the peace and joy of your salvation.

Eternal and ever-living God, may we with [N and] all who have died in the peace of Christ come to the fulfilment of our lives, which is to know you even as we are fully known, and see you face to face in the glory of your kingdom.

In silence let us offer our own prayers to our heavenly Father.

According to the basic threefold pattern

These might be used in a shorter or said service with a silence after each petition and with any appropriate responses, or used in a principal service with one of the suggested sung responses. Again, like those in the fivefold sample sets, any appropriate ending may be used.

Sample set D

Let us pray for the Church and for the world, and let us thank God for his goodness.

God our Father, we thank you for all that you have made, and for your continuing work of creation and re-creation. Hear our prayers for all who exercise authority in human society. May their work be guided by your summons to justice, and your promise of peace. Teach us to share the resources of our planet in fairness and generosity, and work for the good of all people.

Gracious Lord, we thank you for the gift of your Son Jesus, and that through him you call us to a new life in your Church. Hear us as we pray for N our archbishop, N our bishop, and all those whom you give us as teachers and pastors. May they know the strength and wisdom of your Spirit as they do your work. Guide us and all your Church in the ways of faith, hope, and love.

God of compassion, we thank you for the healing ministry of your Son entrusted to your Church. Help us to reach out in care and compassion to all those in need. Calm the minds of the distressed and bring light to those struggling with the darkness of depression. Bring your healing and wholeness to all in need [, especially . . .]. May they know your love and care for them, and find all their needs met by your healing presence with them.

In silence we bring our own prayers before God.

Sample set E

In the power of the Spirit and in union with Christ, let us pray to the Father.

Loving Father, we praise you for your work in the creation of the universe. We hold before you all those scientists and researchers who seek out the knowledge of what you have made: may they be guided by the love of truth. We pray for all those whose power and influence affects the use of their discoveries. May governments and people use the wonders of the world for good purposes, for the feeding of the hungry, the building up of peace, and the healing of the sick.

Giver of life, we thank you for the tender love you revealed to us through the prophets, and made flesh in Jesus your Son. May we know your motherly love in our lives and the life of your Church, as you feed us with your own divine love, truth, and life through him.

Bless *N* our archbishop, Pope Benedict, and all who are called to leadership in your worldwide Church. Draw us closer into unity, so that we may know your love more deeply, and bear a more faithful witness to Jesus through his cross and resurrection.

Living Lord, we give you thanks and praise for your many gifts which enrich our lives. As we remember all those who give their time and talents in faithful service of others, we pray especially for those who work in health care. Strengthen them as they serve you in their fellow human beings in need. We hold before you those in their care, and all people with particular needs [, especially . . .]. Bring them healing, strength, encouragement, and comfort in their troubles, and fill them with the joy of your salvation.

In silence let us offer our own prayers to our heavenly Father.

According to the alternative style

Sample set F

This set uses the response: 'let us pray to the Lord . . ., Lord, have mercy.' The 'Lord, have mercy' could be replaced by a sung Kyrie like the one on page 38. Not every petition need be used on every occasion.

In faith and hope let us pray to the Lord saying: 'Lord, have mercy'.

For *N* our archbishop, *N* and *N* our bishops, and the clergy and people of this diocese, that we may walk faithfully in the footsteps of Christ, let us pray to the Lord . . .

For the unity of the Church throughout the world, and for our brothers and sisters meeting elsewhere this morning, that together our witness may become more faithful, let us pray to the Lord . . .

For those places of the world struggling against tyranny and dictatorship, that God may raise up new prophets, and strengthen all those who thirst for justice, let us pray to the Lord . . .

For all those seeking freedom from violence, in places of war and terror, and in their homes, that God will raise up peacemakers of imagination and compassion, let us pray to the Lord . . .

For our government, and all with responsibility in society, that they may be guided by God's wisdom, and serve the common good, let us pray to the Lord . . .

For all those who work in the media, that they may seek the light of truth in what is news, and what is life-enhancing and joy-bringing in entertainment, let us pray to the Lord . . .

For those who serve in the emergency services, and all those on whom we depend for safety and security, that they too may be kept safe in their service, let us pray to the Lord . . .

For those who administer the law, for those who have committed wrong, and for those in prison, that they may know the justice that restores people, and rights what is wrong, let us pray to the Lord . . .

For those who suffer from mental illness and depression, that they may know the power of God to restore what is broken and bring joy out of sorrow, let us pray to the Lord . . .

For [N, and all] those struggling with illness, or with the afflictions of age, that they may know the strength and healing of Christ's touch, let us pray to the Lord . . .

For [N, and all] those who are mourning and grieving the loss of loved ones, that they may know God as their comforter, let us pray to the Lord . . .

For [N, and all] those who have gone to their rest in the hope of rising again, that God will bring us with them to fullness of life in Christ, let us pray to the Lord . . .

For us, that we may be absolved our sins and offences, and with all the saints follow Christ in the way of holiness, let us pray to the Lord . . .

For all God's creation, that it may come at last to its true fulfilment, and that all people may come into the inheritance of true freedom promised to God's children, let us pray to the Lord . . .

In silence, let us offer our own prayers to the Lord.

Appendix A
An exercise – what's wrong here?

Look at the prayer below and take some time to analyse what works
and what doesn't work.

> Father God, we just come to you in prayer this morning, and
> thank you for all your love for the world, and for the beauty of
> creation. We thank you for the sunshine, and for the rain that
> waters the earth, for the living creatures that bring such
> diversity to our planet. Above all we thank you for your great
> love in coming to suffer and die for us because you loved us
> so much.
>
> Lord, in your mercy
> **hear our prayer.**
>
> Lord, we praise you that you have called us into your Church.
> We pray now for your church in this diocese, and for our
> bishops. We do just pray, Lord, that you will give them wisdom,
> so that they may really come to know you and preach the Word
> in season and out of season, so that all men come to know thee,
> the only God, and Jesus Christ whom thou hast sent.
>
> Lord, in your mercy
> **hear our prayer.**
>
> Almighty and everlasting God, we are so concerned and
> worried by the situation in the Middle East right now. We pray
> that just as you sent the Prince of Peace into the dangers of
> Herod's Bethlehem, so now we really would ask you to bring
> peace to the people of Israel. When we see the little children
> who are killed by these wicked people's suicide bombs, our
> hearts just go out to them, Lord. We really do pray that you
> would show your sovereign arm outstretched over all the
> world, and make people beat their swords into ploughshares,

and their spears into pruning hooks, for Jesus Christ's sake. Amen.

We pray as well for your church here in this place, Lord Jesus. We thank you for the success of our gift day last Saturday. We praise you for the wonderful generosity you inspired in people's hearts, so moving them by your Spirit that they pledged £56,321 to our new youth project. We ask your guidance now for the committee who will be appointing the youth worker. We pray for a man after your own heart, who will reach out to the lost children of this town, and see that the fields are white and ready for harvest.

Lord, in your mercy
hear our prayer.

We remember, Father, how in his lifetime Jesus healed the sick with his loving touch, and we pray for all those who are sick or suffering in any way, that he will just stretch out his mighty hand over all those who lie in their bed of sickness today and bid them rise up and walk. Especially we pray for Jean, as she struggles with her hip problem, and for Dr Smith, and for Jenny as she goes into hospital this week for her hysterectomy. Be with them and everyone else who is suffering, and bless them with the power of your healing.

Lord, in your mercy
hear our prayer.

We thank you for the life of Bert, who was such a wonderful member of our church, and always had time for a word with anyone. We will miss his wisdom, O Lord, but we pray for Mary and his family who will miss him so much more. We ask you to guide our minister, Bob, as he leads that funeral next Wednesday at 10.30, so that he may console the family in their sorrow that Bert has passed into eternal life and joy with you.

Lord, in your mercy
hear our prayer.

So we join our prayers together in the words of the grace:

The grace of our Lord Jesus Christ, the love of God, and the fellowship of the Holy Spirit, be with us all, evermore. Amen.

Appendix B
A workshop event

You may choose to use this booklet as the basis for a parish (or deanery) workshop for those who lead intercessions. This might be for initial or continuing training, for a single or more than one occasion. Here is one possible way of using it.

Workshop 1: Basics

1. Begin by inviting people to buzz with their neighbour about what has helped them or hindered them in the ways other people have led the prayers. Depending on the time available, you may wish to use a plenary session to make a list of these in two columns on a flip-chart.
2. Invite them in small groups to do the exercise 'What's wrong here?' in Appendix A. In a plenary session go through the mistakes identified. There will usually need to be time allowed for some discussion about whether some items are mistakes or not.
3. Explore the basic fivefold pattern in Chapters 3 to 7, and the material on responses in Chapters 13 and 14. (Leave out the section on the alternative pattern and its response.)
4. Finish with the hints and tips in Chapter 19.

Workshop 2: Building blocks

1. Either lead or have someone lead people in a set of prayers that are in the alternative style of biddings as an opening act of worship (for example, drawing on sample set F on page 56).
2. Reflect on the theology of prayer, using Chapter 2 as a guide. How much do people see prayer as a privilege and not simply a task, a calling and not simply a job?
3. Recap conclusions reached in the previous session.
4. Look at the alternative pattern of prayer, using biddings, in Chapter 9. For some people their use at the beginning of the

workshop may have been their first taste of this style of praying. Draw particular attention to the language, especially the danger of using the word 'you' inappropriately.

5. Explore the threefold pattern (Chapter 8), and lead on to ways of doing this with songs. Ideally people should be encouraged to learn some of the typical songs that can be used, so that this part of the workshop is more about experiencing different ways of praying than discussing the theory.

Appendix C

Working with hymns and songs

In Chapter 15 (p. 38) we looked at some of the ways in which music could be used as part of the prayers. One of the possibilities mentioned was the adaptation of songs or hymns. Because this is a more meditative style, and more likely to be used on a special occasion, I have placed a worked example here in an appendix, rather than in the main text which concentrates on the more regular types of worship.

This is an example using F. W. Faber's 'There's a wideness in God's mercy'. This is a hymn that comes in several different versions in different hymnbooks. We are not obliged to use every verse, nor to use them entirely in the order in which they come in any particular book. In fact, virtually all recent hymnbooks omit the opening verses given in older ones as 'Souls of men, why will ye scatter . . .'. The tune also needs some consideration. This hymn can be sung to several different tunes, and for prayer a reasonably reflective tune will be needed, such as 'Cross of Jesus'. Some hymns and songs simply may not lend themselves to this kind of exercise because the tune is too fast-paced or exuberant to be used easily as a prayer response.

Here then is an example of using this hymn as the framework for prayer. Because this is a hymn that is not directly addressed to God, the words of the hymn are not a prayer response. Rather, in this case, our prayers are a response to the teaching expressed in the hymn, as truths about God evoke prayer from us. In deciding how prayer and song relate, it is important to take these sorts of consideration into account.

> There's a wideness in God's mercy,
> like the wideness of the sea;
> there's a kindness in his justice,
> which is more than liberty.

> Gracious God, you invite us to embrace the world in prayer, and so
> share in your love for all you have made, and work with you for the
> coming of your kingdom in all its fullness.

> For the love of God is broader
> than the measure of our mind;
> and the heart of the Eternal
> is most wonderfully kind.

Loving Lord, hear our prayers for your Church, together with
N our bishop, and all in this place. Fill us with your love, that we may
share your kindness in generous open-heartedness as we go about
our daily lives.

> But we make his love too narrow
> by false limits of our own;
> and we magnify his strictness
> with a zeal he will not own.

Forgive us for the way in which we turn your holiness into our own
self-righteousness. Help us to speak up for what is right and true in
ways that serve the liberation of all creation, and bring justice to
those who are oppressed.

> There is no place where earth's sorrows
> are more felt than up in heaven;
> there is no place where earth's failings
> have such kindly judgement given.

We bring to your merciful care all those whose lives are blighted by
sin, sorrow, and suffering. Lift up those who have fallen, strengthen
those who struggle, and give ease and comfort to all who are
distressed.

> There is plentiful redemption
> in the blood that has been shed;
> there is joy for all the members
> in the sorrows of the Head.

Gracious Lord, may the wounded hands of Jesus impart his gracious
healing to those who are sick. May all who find themselves walking
in darkness discover your Christ sorrowing with them, and leading
them towards the light of life.

> 'Tis not all we owe to Jesus;
> it is something more than all;
> greater good because of evil,
> larger mercy through the fall.

Lord of all, enrich our lives with the vision of your goodness, and fill us with gratitude for all you have done for us, that we may more readily live in the light of your goodness and generosity. Help us to journey on in faith and hope, until we see the complete triumph of the cross, and the fullness of the resurrection.

> If our love were but more simple,
> we should take him at his word;
> and our lives would be all gladness
> in the joy of Christ our Lord.

Gracious God, help us indeed to take you at your word, and commend ourselves and all creation to your unfailing love.

Merciful Father . . .

Notes

1 *Common Worship: Christian Initiation*, Church House Publishing, 2006, p. 101.

2 *Common Worship: Services and Prayers for the Church of England*, Church House Publishing, 2000, p. 174. This is the main Sunday services book, and from now on in these notes will simply be referred to as *CW*. Other volumes of *Common Worship* will be specified by name.

3 *CW*, p. 281. This form has a long history, and has evolved gradually over the various stages of liturgical revision and development from the 1960s onwards.

4 The *Kirchentag* is a significant annual ecumenical celebration in the life of the German churches.

5 The phrase 'year's mind' is a traditional way of referring in prayer to the anniversary of someone's death.

6 This prayer can be found in the selection of prayers that follows the Litany.

7 The pattern printed here can be found in *CW*, p. 282.

8 Some examples of a Christmas bidding prayer can be found in *Common Worship: Times and Seasons*, Church House Publishing, 2006, pp. 88–9.

9 The pattern printed here can be found in *CW*, pp. 286–7.

10 This excerpt is the prayer for the world that can be found in *Common Worship: Times and Seasons*, pp. 316–17.

11 *New Patterns for Worship*, Church House Publishing, 2002, second ed. 2009, see especially p. 178 for examples, and the pages that follow for full sample sets of prayers.

12 There are examples of prayer addressed to Jesus in *New Patterns for Worship,* such as those on pp. 195–6 and 206–7.

13 This is an often repeated saying especially popular with singers and musicians. It is attributed to St Augustine and seems to be a summary based on his exposition of Psalm 73 (72): 'For he that sings praise not only praises, but praises with gladness: he that sings praise not only sings, but also loves him of whom he sings. In praise, there is the speaking forth of one confessing; in singing, the affection of one loving' (*Augustine on Psalm 73.1,* http:// www.newadvent.org/fathers/1801073.htm).

14 *New Patterns for Worship,* pp.179–80.

15 By Daniel Iverson, as found, for example, in *Mission Praise* 613.

16 Sixth century by Venantius Fortunatus, as in, for example, *New English Hymnal* 79.

17 By Graham Kendrick, as in, for example, *Complete Anglican Hymns Old and New* 60.

18 In *CW,* p. 289, with some other possible endings for the prayers.

19 The obvious introductory starting point is Sue Wallace, *Multi-sensory Prayer,* Scripture Union, 2004.

20 *Common Worship: Daily Prayer,* Church House Publishing, 2005, particularly the resource section of prayers on pp. 360–409.